Recsive' ... Dorice 3·4·10

Donal

was

from Peru. IN

MW01295442

Martha Sue 3-5-10
Gene 3-5-10

A Shout-out to the Youth of America

"A Guide for Fathers"

An introduction to "Don the Dad"
The Divine M.O.F.I.A. (Men of Faith in America)
The United Shades of America
and Operation Peace and Brotherhood

Donald R. Fuller Sr.

Acknowledgements

First and foremost I would like to thank my Heavenly Father and Lord and Savior Jesus Christ. Thank you for your blessings, grace and mercy. Thank you for revealing to me the fullness of your redemptive powers.

I thank my Mother for the Faith and Love that she has always shown me.

I thank my family for having Love and patience with me while I have worked on writing this book and the project that I will present to you.

I thank my former co-workers also for having Faith in me, and helping me to fulfill a dream.

Thank you Jim, you are Godsend and have become a true Soul Brother.

Thank you Tyrone for keeping me "pumped" and strong in my Faith.

"All of us are born for a reason, but not all of us discover why. Success in life has nothing to do with what you gain in life or accomplish for yourself, it is what you do for others." Author unknown

"We must develop and maintain the capacity to forgive. He who is devoid of the power to forgive is devoid of the power to Love."
Dr. Martin Luther King Jr.

"The very difficulty of a problem evokes abilities or talents which would otherwise, in happy times, never emerge or shine."
Horace

"I refuse to accept the view that mankind is so tragically bound to the starless midnight of racism and war that the bright daybreak of Peace and Brotherhood can never become a reality."
Dr. Martin Luther King Jr.

Foreword

No malice is intended at all by what you will read in this instruction manual. I call it an instruction manual and not a book because it really is information about mentoring to, and helping the youth of our community, other cities in the state, and all across the nation.

I want the youth of our country, and particularly their dad's or male members in their families to try to embrace and engage in the theories and activities that will be presented to them in this manual.

At this writing, there are so many problems and woes in our country.

There is so much bitterness, distrust and hate.

My friends and fellow Americans feel and see all of the lies and deceit, locally, regionally, and nationally and are very upset, disillusioned, and feel helpless.

Issues are discussed daily by common citizens around the water cooler, in ballparks, gymnasiums and in our homes, but many feel that all they can do is just talk about the issues, and that the "powers that be" do not care enough to change the situation.

We all recognize the nepotism and favoritism that is practiced daily, but feel helpless and prostrate.

In this instruction manual I share with you the raw, naked truth!

Once again I say no malice is intended, but it is the truth!

It is often said that "the truth will set you free!"

If we are to truly see each other as Brothers and Sisters.

If we truly do care for ALL of our youth, regardless of their race or creed or social status, then we must accept the truth and move on.

I have done that in spite of many years of anger and some very difficult times.

If there is any doubt about that, please read this instruction manual.

After you have read it, please understand that you would not have had the opportunity to read it had I not been able to let go of all of the hate and bitterness that I will describe to you.

I feel nothing but Peace, Brotherhood and Love for everyone that I ever considered an enemy or a foe, and sincerely hope that they feel the same way towards me.

I hope that they will help me mentor to the youth of our community and country.

Rich or poor, black or white, when you all live in the same community, you all share the same joy and pain.

You become family, and it truly does take a village to raise our youth today.

An introduction to Faith based initiatives for the youth of America and the youth of the World

This project in every sense of the word is based on Faith. When you unleash the power of Faith, anything and everything is possible.

Once in a Blue Moon the political powers in our nation's capitol and corporate America get things right.

They sometimes realize that our government is intended to be about the people, and for the people, not self-serving.

They sometimes realize that it must be all inclusive.

It is my sincere desire that this project will turn our nation's capitol upside down, and the powers that be in Washington D.C. and on Wall Street will make the welfare of our youth and all common citizens one of the top priorities in this country.

This project is dedicated to my family, my brothers and, sisters, my friends, and most importantly to my Mother. They have always had Faith in me, and I wish to share that Faith with you.

Faith is God's source of power that he freely gives to anyone who believes.

This project is especially developed for the youth of our country.

Their lives are changing so rapidly, and I feel that my generation and the "powers that be" in our country are not doing an adequate job in addressing the issues that challenge not only our youth, but all of us.

I sincerely hope that this project will open many eyes, and change many hearts and minds.

The United Shades of America is A New Generation of Hope.

Operation Peace and Brotherhood is not just an act, it's an attitude!

Contents:

The United Shades of America

A Faith based initiative presented to the youth of America. They are one of our country's greatest natural resources.

When we make their morals, welfare, education and recreation one of the top priorities in this country, we will be investing wisely in our futures.

Operation Peace and Brotherhood

A Faith based initiative presented to my fellow citizens of America and the World.

We have the power through Faith to bring about a positive change in the lives of our youth, our country and the world.

Touching letters

A few letters written by faculty and students to whom I have spoken throughout the years.

They capture the Soul and Spirit in which this project was conceived and produced.

The Divine M.O.F.I.A. LLC
Men of Faith in America

The Divine M.O.F.I.A. (Men of Faith in America) is a new organization of men and women of Faith in America who will mentor to the needs of the youth of our country.

One of the primary missions of the organization is to feed, read and provide means of exercise to the youth in our community and other cities across the nation.

For over twenty-five years, I have read to and spoken to thousands of students about the virtues of Peace and Brotherhood, and tolerance and acceptance.

A few years ago, the Human Resources Manager of an International Automotive supplier who happened to have a facility located in my hometown, contacted me and asked if they could assist me with the reading program that I had initiated.

They helped supply books and volunteers to read to the students, and as a result of our efforts, there are over one-hundred volunteers who read to students in K-4th grade in our county every January.

All of the 5th grade students in our county are shown a video entitled "My Friend Martin".

It is a video about the life and legacy of Rev. Dr. Martin Luther King Jr.

I speak to all of the 6th grade students in the county about the virtues of Peace and Brotherhood, and tolerance and acceptance.

For the past two years there has been a joint effort by our local school system and our local YMCA to feed students during the summer while school is not in session. Without this feeding program, there would be some students who would not have an opportunity to eat breakfast and lunch during the summer.

It is a goal of The Divine M.O.F.I.A. to help enhance and expand both of the aforementioned programs.

Additionally there are many projects and programs that we envision the Divine M.O.F.I.A. assisting with in the creation and funding aspects.

I will attempt to reach out to as many students as I can through a book (instruction manual) that I have written titled *A Shout-out to the Youth of America, "A Guide for Fathers."*

A percentage from the sales of this book will be used to help fund the feeding and reading programs and other projects that we hope to initiate in the community.

I have spoken with many of the men and women in the community, and we are in total agreement that there needs to be more activities for ALL of our youth to be involved in.

We have been brainstorming about the following projects:

- An indoor practice facility for youth football, baseball, and soccer
- Indoor batting cages
- A miniature golf course
- A skating rink
- A bank of computers/education center
- A food court
- A drill/marching team

I encourage ALL men in America to consider the dynamics of this project.

There are tangible things that we can do right now by taking responsibility for our own kids, and their friends and playmates.

We must all realize that a positive change begins in our own homes.

As I pass out preliminary business cards, I encourage men to put the cards next to credit cards in their wallets.

Whenever they use a credit card for a purchase that they may desire for themselves, I encourage them to think about their children also.

As this project develops, there will be a website that will contain helpful information for men and their families concerning their health, nutrition, education and other resources that will help them more effectively mentor to our youth.

Until this project is fully developed, I ask you to please keep the Faith!

Sponsored by

The Divine M.O.F.I.A. LLC

Men of Faith in America

dfuller_76@yahoo.com

729 W. Albert Dr.

Peru, In 46970

630-303-4627

Youth Mentors

Human Rights and Social Justice Advocates

Biography

Who I am

I am a husband, a father, a son, a brother, an uncle, a nephew and a friend.

I have a vested interest in this project because I have a family also, and my daughters' and sons' friends are my friends also. I consider them my daughters and sons too.

If we provide them all with a stable home and mentor to them, they can all reach their potential and become stars or productive members of society.

I care deeply about their futures, and I am trying to raise my daughters and sons, and their friends to believe in the values and virtues that I will try to express through this project.

My wife and I have been married for three decades, and have two daughters, three sons and a grandson.

My daughters and sons were born in four different decades.

A daughter and two sons are adults.

My wife is my father-in-law's namesake. My oldest daughter is my sister-in-laws namesake. My oldest son is my brothers (best friend) namesake. My middle son is my father-in-laws namesake. My youngest son is my namesake. My youngest son is my grandson's uncle, and they are the same age. My youngest daughter was born on my birthday.

My family is very special to me.

My Mother was employed by our State, has been honored by our <u>State and City</u> and has been retired for two decades.

My father was employed by our city, and has been deceased for four decades.

I was born in a railroad town in the Midwest in the late fifties.

There was a military installation in my hometown also.

I had four older sisters, (one a twin) a younger sister, and three older brothers.

My oldest brother and sister were much older, and lived out of State.

My other six siblings and I were only separated by seven years in age. We were all very close; in age and spirit.

My oldest sister at home was very special. She was born with a heart condition, an enlarged heart. My special sister really did have a big heart, and she touched all of our lives very deeply.

Childhood

We had no video games, computers, cell phones or other electronics gadgets when we were growing up, but we had each other.

Since our hometown was a railroad and military town, in addition to my siblings, there was always an abundance of playmates.

We ran and played outside from sun up until dark, and only went inside when the street light had been on for quite awhile.

Our playmates were of various races and nationalities, and for the most part there was peace and harmony among the youth in our neighborhood.

Sometimes the adults in our community though, would hold on to an antebellum way of thinking, and there would be racial strife.

My Special Sister

My special sister was viciously beaten by a group of other girls when she was twelve years old.

They beat her because she was different, and they just didn't understand.

The beating left my sister speechless and paralyzed. She had to be placed in a nursing home at the age of twelve.

No criminal charges were pursued.

My Mother allowed me to visit and read to my sister often.

My father passed away just months after the incident, and just short of his fiftieth birthday.

My special sister was twelve years old, my youngest sister was only six years old, and my twin and I were seven years old when my father passed away.

My Mother was a widow with seven daughters and sons and she was only three and a half decades old.

My mother did not even drive, but she continued to work for the State and take care of my special sister and my siblings and me.

We all remained stable, and close.

We watched my special sister's health decline though.

My sister passed away in the nursing home at the age of fourteen.

I was very young (seven) when my father passed away, and it was hard for me to comprehend the difference between passed-away and passed-out.

I learned a lot in two short years because when my sister was called home, I knew she had passed-away.

A Star in the Making

My oldest brother living at home was ten when my father passed away, and was his namesake.

He was the **best** natural athlete that I have ever seen in my life, and I have been blessed enough athletically to have been around and competed against pro athletes.

At **eleven years old** my brother was competitively playing sandlot baseball and basketball against nineteen and twenty-year old men.

Because of his superior natural skills, he would always be one of the first players picked.

The opposing players would threaten to beat him up if he hit a home run. His teammates would threaten to beat him up if he did not hit a home run.

He would hit a home run, and as he rounded third base he would hurdle the fence and run to our house, three blocks away from the ball park.

My Best Friend

I had another brother who was just a year older then my twin and I, and was born on Christmas Day. He and I did everything together. He was my best friend. We were both very athletic also, but he cared more about music and art.

We both marveled at our older brother's athleticism.

When my brother (best friend) and twin were wrestling one day, he fell and broke his arm. As a result of the injury, he missed time in school and was held back in the second grade. He became classmates with my twin and me.

My oldest remaining sister at home took care of me and my other siblings during the summers while my Mother worked.

She is an excellent seamstress, and taught us all how to sew. My Mother taught us all how to knit.

In spite of what we had been through, we were a tight knit family, thanks to my Mother's Faith and a great support system of neighbors, friends and relatives who also lived in the neighborhood.

My Family and I were all in the house together every evening, crowded around, and watching the only television set that we had.

We did not have a lot of material possessions, but again, we had each other.

My Best Friend is Gone...

My family was suddenly shaken to the very core when I was thirteen years old.

There was a racially tinged murder in my hometown, and as a result, a state policeman was shot and killed before the suspect was eventually cornered and burned alive.

Four months later, my brother; my best friend, was poisoned to death.

That diabolic incident changed the innocence of my family forever.

My Mother showed so much grace and dignity throughout that horrific time that I can not even begin to describe or explain it.

She stoically said that nothing would bring my brother back and that we must go on and live our lives.

Once again, no criminal charges were pursued.

My Superstar Brother

My other brother was sixteen years old at the time.

He had unbelievable athletic ability, as I have said, but after losing his father and sister, and now a brother by such a cruel and callous act, he desperately needed a male mentor in his life.

That mentor turned out to be his high school basketball coach.

My older brother had bragged to me and my brother that he was going to start on the varsity basketball team the following season.

We knew that he was good, but that was an incredible boast considering that our high school had just graduated an All-American basketball player who went on to play college basketball, and eventually in the pros.

When my brother was in middle school, he beat a twenty-one year old man in a game of one-on-one and bragged about it. The man got mad and beat him up with a dog chain.

My Mother invited the man's brother over for Thanksgiving dinner the following week.

She is so forgiving and understanding.

My brother came off of the bench in his first varsity game and had over twenty points and fifteen rebounds.

A Star was born, and my other brother, my best friend; would never know!

Basketball was (is) huge in the Midwest, especially in my home state.

There were (are) basketball hoops inside and outside of homes.

Many pro players were (are) developed in our area and state.

The basketball court was the perfect place for my brother to express himself and release some of the frustrations that had grown in his heart.

He had a great sophomore year and (in spite of a new coach) junior year, and became a starter and averaged a double-double.

He was ambidextrous and could stand underneath the basket and jump and put his elbow on the rim.

During a game one time, an opposing player tried to take a charge on him. He jumped over the other player and laid it in.

Division one schools contacted my brother. My brother's mentor and coach would call our house at night to make sure that he was not a part of the typical mischief that our youth get into.

His mentor and coach got fired after his sophomore year due to small-town politics.

A New Basketball Coach
Comes to Town

A new basketball coach came to town.

My brother had an abundance of raw talent, and desperately needed a coach and mentor to help him hone his basketball skills, but the new coach had his own agenda.

He had a son who he wanted to be Mr. Basketball in our state, and eventually play college and pro basketball.

When I say that if we have Faith and mentor to our youth and make their morals, welfare, recreation, and educational needs a priority in this country and they will succeed, **I really mean it.** I experienced that first hand with the new coach.

He mentored to, and coached his son and a select few other players, including a state legend's son to perfection.

His son became an excellent basketball player as a result.

The legend's son was not from our home town, but my brother was.

The legend's son already had a mentor, his father. My brother lost his twice now.

My brother had more natural talent then the coaches' son, a fact that can not be denied, and was arguably the best athlete ever at our school.

Had my brother continued to be mentored to and coached, his possibilities on the basketball court were unlimited; he could have been a pro.

The new coach had a brilliant basketball mind and certainly deserved to be elected to the state basketball hall of fame based on his knowledge of the game.

He just failed to spread the blessings of his knowledge, coaching, and mentoring to ALL others and not just a select few.

I promised myself that no child would ever be left behind ever again if I could do anything to help.

The new coach achieved all of the goals that he had set for himself when he became the coach at our school.

His son won the Mr. Basketball award, he deserved it; he was tough!

I witnessed the verbal and physical abuse he took from opposing players and sometimes his own teammates because he was a "coach's son".

His son played division one basketball.

His son won a NCAA Basketball National Championship.

His son played pro basketball.

The new coach and son were elected to the State Basketball Hall of Fame.

My brother lost his coach and mentor though, and ultimately his dream.

He had too much talent and it got in the way of the new coaches' agenda.

His dreams were deferred when he got into trouble and was suspiciously and maliciously not allowed to play basketball his senior year.

He was blessed when other men in the community stepped up and assisted in his effort to play Division-Two basketball, which he did.

His spirit was broken however, and he never did reach his full potential.

He passed away a decade ago from a broken heart, barely four decades old.

I Could Hoop Too

I was three years younger then my brother, and I continued to play basketball. I was not as athletically gifted as my brother, but I certainly could hold my own on the basketball court and in other sports.

My brother could stand right underneath the basket and jump and put his elbow on the rim, as I have stated.

I could put my elbow on the rim too, but I had to have a running start.

My brother was ambidextrous, I was not, so he could handle the basketball much better than I could.

I played with the coach's son for three years.

I cracked the starting line-up six games into my junior year, and remained in the starting line-up the rest of my high school career.

My junior year I was the only underclassman on a team full of seniors, including the coaches' son.

I endured a measurable amount of harassment for a number of different reasons, including the fact that I was the only underclassman on the varsity squad.

The coaches' son averaged thirty-five shots and thirty-five points a game in his senior year, and did win the state's Mr. Basketball award.

We all played in the coach's son's shadow; rarely did any other player shoot the ball more then ten or fifteen times a game.

My senior year was very gratifying because the coaches' son had graduated, and I was able to freely shoot ten to fifteen times a game. I averaged over twenty points a game.

I had more freedom on the basketball court, led our team in scoring and was voted most valuable player.

I was the second leading scorer in our conference, and made first-team all conference, after receiving no mention at all the previous year.

My brother and me, and many others experienced nepotism and favoritism.

I share this story with you, once again not out of malice, but because they are facts that my family and the community have lived with for many years.

We must be all inclusive when we mentor to our youth today.

If we intentionally over look one, we all suffer in one way or another.

It is often said that life isn't fair, and that may be true.

We must not allow the fact that life isn't fair sometimes, to beoame an excuse or reason to not make an honest effort to treat each other fair.

It is often said too, that what goes around, comes around...

Track

Athletics were an important part of our lives when we were growing up.

As I stated earlier, we always ran and played outside most of our free time.

There is no doubt in my mind that all of the running and bike riding that we did growing up, really helped to develop our muscles.

My brother and I had some "serious hops!"

I ran track also, and set the school record in the high-jump my junior year with a leap of six-feet eight inches.

I went to the State track meet where I finished in eighth place in the high jump.

I made all-state in track my senior year after finishing sixth in the high-jump at the state track meet.

The United States Air Force

I really had no desire to attend college right out of high school, so I joined the United States Air Force instead, at the age of eighteen.

I was an enlisted airman, stationed on a pilot training base in the Southwest United States.

I was assigned to the Civil Engineering Squadron, and played basketball for the squadron and base basketball teams.

I enjoyed my time in the Air Force, particularly traveling all over the Southwest and playing basketball against players from other bases, and against college teams who had campuses nearby.

I met pilots and other military personnel from all over the world.

It helped to fuel my deep belief that basically we are all the same.

We all want safety and security and comfort for our families.

I particularly enjoyed meeting people from other countries.

It was always interesting to hear their views about The United States of America.

One of the more interesting people that I met was a Crown Prince from the Middle East.

My Mother always taught us to treat people the same regardless of their social status or lack of.

That is the way I have always tried to treat others, including the Crown Prince.

Others were in awe of the Prince, or maybe understood protocol better then I, but I just saw another young man (I was twenty at the time) who was different than me and I wanted to learn more about him.

He spoke to me first, and as we would talk, his bodyguards would just walk off into the distance a bit, knowing that I was no threat to the Prince.

Again, that helps to fuel my belief that basically we are all the same.

I had a really wonderful productive career in the Air Force while I was stationed in the Southwest. I made rank very quickly.

I was honored as Wing Airman of the Month on two different occasions.

I was honored with a special day on two different occasions by the city the Air Force base was located in.

I was offered a few Division-One scholarships to play basketball, as my Air Force enlistment was nearing it's end.

The Southwest part of the country was more football country than it was basketball at the time, so I decided to return to the Midwest to attend college and play basketball.

You can never go Home Again

There were some very wise older gentlemen who were military veterans and they warned me that, "you can never go home again!"

They told me that I had grown into a man, and that I would see life much differently when I returned to my hometown.

I wanted to go back to the Midwest to attend college and play basketball.

I needed to go back to my hometown to help my family.

I went home after my initial enlistment, and I joined the Air Force Reserves, and started taking college courses until I could enroll on campus as a full time student when the semester ended.

Sudden Change in Plans

While I was waiting for the semester to end, I met my future wife on a blind date.

I fell in love and started a family.

I continued to take college courses, but I never did pursue my dream of playing college basketball.

I loved my wife and family more then I loved basketball. I could not believe it because my brother and I lived and breathed basketball.

I have told you already how unique my family is.

At this writing, my daughters and sons range in age from twenty-nine through age seven.

I am sure that anyone who has children knows that it takes time, patience, money, and you sacrifice a lot of things.

I have always had more time and patience than money, but we have always found a way to make things work.

In our three decades of marriage, there have been many trials and tribulations also, but we have always found a way to make things work.

My Local Job

Two weeks before I graduated from high school, my drafting teacher and a guidance counselor, two great mentors of mine, procured a job for me.

I was hired as a draftsman at a local electrical distribution company.

I worked for two months, and was offered permanent employment, but I had already made up my mind that I was going to join the Air Force in the fall.

When I returned to my home town after my enlistment, I was rehired by the company as a draftsman.

The wisdom of the older gentlemen who warned me that, "you can never go home again" came to light as I began my new job.

It became obvious to all of my co-workers that I was different than they were.

I had a very passionate belief that ALL people should be treated fair and equal.

Although my co-workers did not necessarily share my same beliefs or the passion that I held for equality, most did respect me and my views.

I learned a lot from my co-workers, and they learned a lot from me.

Contract Work

After eight years on the job, the company decided to relocate the Engineering department to the Southeastern part of the United States.

I was very actively coaching in youth baseball leagues in our area, so I chose not to relocate, and I acquired a contract job designing audio systems for a major United States automotive supplier.

I worked with Engineers from all over the world, including the Middle East, and the Far East.

We were all casual but professional, and got along very well together. That further validated in my mind, that basically we are all the same.

When my contract with the automotive supplier expired, I procured briefly a contract as a Process Engineer with another automotive supplier.

I was responsible for plant layout design, and locating and documenting the placement of robotic equipment.

My Local Job, the Sequel

The contract expired after six months, and I returned to the electrical distribution company, as they were restarting the Engineering department.

When I returned to the company for the third time, there had been major changes in management.

One of my former co-workers was my manager now, and he did not share my passion or belief that everyone should be treated fair and equal.

We got along very well when we were contemporaries, but he, like others sometimes, had difficulty handling authority because he was not properly prepared for the task at the time.

He viewed me as a token, and made me one of his targets.

He wanted me and my co-workers to fear him more than he wanted us to respect him.

It did not take him long to let me know that he was the one in charge.

On my second day back with the company, he cussed me out and put me down within ear shot of an office full of my co-workers.

At first I thought it was a joke until I saw that neither he, nor anyone else was laughing.

There were times that he would treat me very decent, but he would make certain comments later that let me know that he really did not believe that all people should be treated equal and fair.

The situation only got worse as I became more involved with activities in the community.

I have always had a strong commitment to the youth in our community, and I have been a member of several boards and organizations.

I have coached my daughters and sons and their friends in various sports for over twenty-five years.

I love mentoring to our young.

None of my outside activities ever interfered with my job duties or performance in any way, but my manager told me that I needed to mind my own business and quit trying to act like I was the community savior.

That was particularly upsetting to me because the manager did not even live in or contribute anything to our community.

I continued to perform my tasks at a level equal to, or exceeding my peers, but I was denied promotions, and sent out of state on unnecessary business trips.

My co-workers witnessed the unfortunate situation for several years, but were fearful of losing their own jobs, and would not address the issue.

I started receiving very low reviews on my job performance, and was being set-up to be terminated.

I protected myself and my family by informing human resources, the plant manager, the corporate human resources manager, the president of the company, a State and Federal agency, and my Congressman.

An investigation was conducted by the company, and there was no satisfactory resolution, but I was reassigned to another department working predominately with hourly workers.

That was a total blessing!

The company totally restructured management after my complaints, but never acknowledged the mistreatment that I endured.

Who can Help (?)

The state agency investigating my complaint made a complete mockery of the bureaucratic and judicial process.

I had filed charges with the agency, and waited over five years for a resolution.

When the state investigator arrived at our company to investigate my complaints, his ten year old son was with him.

He left his son sitting in his car on a hot summer day.

He never interviewed me.

He determined that my complaints had no merit.

The investigator was very unprofessional, so I was not surprised.
I was just happy to be away from a dreadful situation, and I learned a lot from my new hourly co-workers.

As the days and weeks and years passed, the situation improved greatly.

What a Blessing

I won a corporate alliance award for community service.

Our company won a national award for excellence in manufacturing.

I mentioned the fact that my new co-workers were hourly because I was salaried, and often times we let our differences get in the way of what could be meaningful friendships.

That never was an issue with my new co-workers, and after years of the torment that I had endured in the office, the treatment I received in a factory setting was refreshing and enlightening.

My hourly co-workers have been a tremendous source of support as I have completed the project that I am presenting.

They shared great resource material with me, material that I did not have time to review adequately when we were co-workers because we all worked so many long hours.

I was one of the millions of Americans who lost their job last year.

Although it really hurts me not to see my former co-workers daily, support them, and they support me, this has turned into a true blessing because it has given me the opportunity to complete this project for the youth of America, a vision that I have shared with my co-workers for many years.

It took me a long time, but I have forgiven my former manager.

He is a father, just like I am a father.

I think that we both ultimately realized that our youth were more important than stroking our own egos.

Now that I have joined my Mother in the Spiritual world (my Mother is still very much alive, and continues to impart her Faith, wisdom and understanding on anyone who will willingly look and listen) I can see so clearly now how she has been able to be so graceful, dignified and understanding all of her life.

It has all been through her **Faith!**

I hope all of you will forgive me for the lack of respect that I may have shown you throughout the years.

We can all be very IGNORANT at times when it comes to understanding one another.

My new hourly co-workers embraced me with open arms, and we became Brothers and Sisters.

They too helped to fuel my belief that basically we are all the same. We all want safety, security and happiness for our families.

I have always just wanted to be free.

I now realize that when you hate others, they control you.

I now realize that when you are blessed with love in your heart and not hate...

YOU TRULY ARE FREE!!!

The United Shades of America

It shouldn't matter whether you are
Black, White, Hispanic, Asian, African,
Indian, Eskimo or whatever; we are all
brothers and sisters!

Not everyone in America is down with this theory or truth, but there are enough who are to make it worth the time and effort to help the *United Shades of America* become a reality...

The flag represents soldiers returning home from war, returning to their children; the youth who we have helped mentor to while their dads and moms, brothers and sisters, aunts and uncles sacrificed so much of their lives serving and protecting our great nation.

It is very important that every youth feel, know and believe that they can be a star and achieve any of the goals that they set in life.

What It Is

The concept for this design was conceived because I can envision a time in this country when we all finally realize that there are all different skin shades of very patriotic, productive citizens in this country. We all have more in common then not, and no one race should, nor does have absolute power in this country anymore.

I can envision a time in this country when we all finally realize that it is because of our wide diversity, not in spite of it, that we have been such a strong nation and a world leader since our independence.

I can envision a time in this world when all other countries view our country in a more positive light and finally realize and believe that our country is not just about the United States of America and it's (sic) sometimes condescending, self-serving politicians, but about the UNITED state of PEOPLE also!

The fact that there are very negative views of the United States of America held by many other countries all around the world should and must not be denied or ignored.

We have the ability and desire to change those perceptions/ realities as demonstrated by the excitement and energy generated in our country during the past Presidential elections.

One of the current Presidential administration's mantras is to "rebuild the country from the ground up". That must include all of the youth of America, because they truly are our country's greatest natural resources.

When we make their morals, recreation, education and welfare one of the top priorities in this country, we are investing wisely in our future and may be less inclined to send them off to fight undefined or unnecessary wars.

We will stop outsourcing and sending their future jobs over seas, and stop the corporate greed.

We will help them define the new jobs of the future that ever changing technology will present to them, and educate and mentor to them so they are prepared to perform those tasks.

The United States of America was conceived from the dreams and desires of freedom and democracy.

It has passed the infancy and adolescence stages, but it is still just an idea and a dream; a work in progress. *The United Shades of America* can help speed up the day when freedom and democracy in this country is a reality for one and all, and not just a wish or a dream.

If this is to become a great nation, this must become true!

Why It Is

I want to honor and thank all of the students and citizens who I have spoken to about the importance of civil and human rights over the past twenty-five years.

Symbolic of their likeness on the stars, I want the students to know that each and every one of them is special, and that they all can figuratively and literally be a star.

I want the gift of this concept to all of the students and citizens of America to be reflective of the efforts of not only myself and what I have tried to convey to everyone who I have spoken to throughout the years, but also all of the other like-minded brothers and sister out there of all races, who are making an effort to help bring about peace, harmony and understanding.

The Seven Pillars

These are seven important lessons that I had to learn in my life the hard way.

I call them pillars because our youth can use these pillars as a foundation to build their lives on. Nothing changes if nothing changes, and change can start right now with each and every one of us if we:

- Give our youth the knowledge and techniques to abstain from sex.

- Realize that we all have problems, and that we all will throughout our entire lives.

- Choose Faith over fear.

- Realize that time and our lives are two of our most valuable possessions, but time is neutral and we only have one life to live, not nine.

- Find a mentor/leader or be one.

- Realize that you cannot control what others say or do but you can control what you say and do.

- Realize that it is all about HUMAN RIGHTS.

Give our youth the knowledge and techniques to abstain from sex.

If we don't get to the point where we are comfortable talking openly and honesty to our youth about sex and abstinence, someone else might talk to them, and they may not have our youth's best interest in their hearts and minds.

Explain to them that there are grown men and women who are still not emotionally ready for sex.

Encourage our sons and daughters to stop putting peer pressure on each other by out-casting and ostracizing their peers who have "never kissed or made out before."

Teach our youth the difference between Love and lust.

Explain that the true meaning behind love is doing for, and helping others.

Explain to them that lust is trying to

always satisfy your own needs, with very little care or concern for others.

Explain to them that true Love is satisfying and gratifying and not pain filled.

Explain to them that lust will leave them feeling empty, lonely and bitter.

Let them know that when they are emotionally ready, love and a true, meaningful relationship are true blessing, but that they will miss out on the blessing if they are blinded by their desire for instant gratification.

Please explain to them that **good things really do come to those who wait!**

Realize that we all have problems, and that we always will throughout our lives.

Explain to our youth that we all have problems in our lives, and we will continue to throughout our lives. The key is how we handle and resolve those problems.

We started learning how to solve problems on our first day of school.

Life is about living and learning by solving problems, big and small.

Problems challenge us and help us to grow spiritually and intellectually.

As we confront our problems openly and honestly, we gain courage and knowledge.

Faith versus Fear

When I speak to students at various schools, I am cognizant of the fact that there is separation of church and state, and that I cannot freely talk about religion or God.

Time is of the essence, so there is no desire to debate that mandate here, but I honestly do believe that separation of church and state has done more harm than good in our school systems and society.

There have been many false prophets and corrupt religious leaders all throughout the history of our nation and mankind. It is not difficult to understand why it is so hard for so many to have Faith, and instead live their lives as slaves to fear.

It is important to understand that we all act naturally in Faith or fear. The two are very closely related, in fact, they are almost identical. They work the same way, but they produce opposite results.

Faith produces love, fear produces hate.

Faith is living life, fear is death in life. We respond to both with certain actions. With Faith, positive words and deeds, with fear, negative words and deeds.

Faith is a force that we must use also, as we reach out to each other in peace and understanding, and mentor to and educate our youth.

Fear is a force that must be overcome in each and every one of us. Only then it will be easier to accept one another as brothers and sisters.

Faith is like your muscles, if you don't use them, they become weak and useless to you. Just as with your muscles you must use your Faith to keep it strong.

We are all born with a natural fear. As babies we jumped at unfamiliar sounds or shied away from strangers.

We can and must positively overcome the kind of fears that have separated us and held us back.

I encourage everyone to explore the dynamics and learn more about Faith verses fear.

Faith truly is the essence of our being, and a spiritual force that cannot be denied. Faith is the substance of things hoped for, and the evidence of things not yet seen to the physical eye.

Students, be prepared, not scared!

Realize that time and our lives are two of our most valuable possessions, but time is neutral and we only have one life to live, not nine.

No matter how rich or poor we are, when we are lying on our death bed, one thing that we desire most is more time. We will not have it then, but we have it now.

Time is neutral. We can use it wisely in a positive manner, or we can do nothing with it or use it in a destructive manner.

There is time for Faith, education, recreation, relaxation. What we get from each of those is determined by the time we put into each of them.

To our students: While you are entertaining yourselves with the latest electronic games and gadgets, your contemporaries overseas are designing those devices and making a lucrative living off of your recreational addictions.

Take time to study and learn more about math and science so you can design your own games and help secure your own future, and in the rebirth of America.

Take time to learn more about your ancestry and other cultures. You cannot know where you are going if you don't know where you are coming from.

Visit a nursing home and talk to the residents. They are living History lessons.

We must know and understand our own history or it will continue to repeat itself in a negative way.

Find a Mentor/Leader or be one

Lead, follow or get the apathy out of the way. Many changes need to be made in this country, and there is no time for grandstanding or worrying about who should get credit for what.

We all must work together in faith and harmony if we are to make this country and world a better place for one and all.

Positive change **must begin in OUR HOMES.**

What we put into the hearts and minds of our young at home will produce what they put out into the streets and schools of our society.

If we make the morals, welfare, education and recreation of our youth a priority in this country, then every child in America could and would have adult mentors in their lives consistently.

Fathers, brothers, uncles; and equally as important, teachers and coaches can and need to be mentoring to our young. If there is a home in this country, where there is only one or no parent involved in the Youth's life, then the village must step up and see to it that the youth's needs are met.

Men, be **MEN**. Take responsibility for not only your children, but for your children's friends also. Take them to a gym, the park, fishing or another activity, but do it on a regular basis. Teach them how to manage a home and finances; life survival skills that help to build self-esteem.

Talk straight across to them, not down to them; they are human too!

Men teach your sons that females are more than just sex objects. Teach them to respect their mothers, sisters, and aunts, and then they will more likely have respect for YOUR mothers, sisters, aunts and daughters!

Teach them about Fredrick Douglass. Regardless of your race or creed, he exuded strength and courage, something confusing to our youth today.

Mothers teach your daughters how to be proper ladies and have respect for their bodies, minds and souls. Teach them about the heroine Harriett Tubman. Her story is one that everyone can be inspired by. It is very true that behind every great man, there is a woman.

Mothers, when and where men won't step up, you must. Please know that unearned suffering is redemptive!

We have to show our youth that real heroes are right in their own homes and communities and not out there in the sports world or in Hollywood.

Realize that you cannot control what others say or do but you can control whatever you say and do

You cannot control the things that other people will say or do to you, but you can control what you say and do to other people. **Take responsibility for your own actions!**

We have all suffered unfair or unjust treatment in the past. That is just a sad reality of living life, but we all must take responsibility for our own actions without making up excuses or blaming others for our woes.

An excuse is nothing more than a lie, wrapped around a reason anyway!

"Sticks and stones may break your bones" but don't ever let evil words hurt you.

Have self-esteem. Believe in yourself, because you can believe that whoever it is who is calling you names or putting you down does not have self-esteem. When you feel good about yourself, you lift others up, not put them down.

Do not spend time or energy arguing or fighting with people who just want to pull you down, not lift you up.

We all have the power within us to make a positive change.

Treat others the way that you want to be treated. That is one of the *"golden rules"* that has been recited and taught for many generations.

It is preached a lot more then it is practiced. It is a simple and basic concept until we make it complicated with exceptions and put our own spin on it. I WILL TREAT OTHERS THE WAY THAT I WANT TO BE TREATED. That is something tangible that we all can start doing right now to help bring about a positive change in this country.

Do something nice for someone without

them even knowing it.

Three of the most powerful and disarming words in our English language are **please** and **thank you**. Those words are double edged. They show respect and they command respect.

You have to give respect in order to get respect.

It is All about Human Rights

There are not any humans alive today that can say that they told their parents that they were ready or wanted to be born. None of us is here by our own volition. We all should have basic human rights, among those to be treated *equal* and *fair.* When we ALL do not have those rights, our own rights are in peril too.

"We hold these truths to be self evident that all men are created equal..."

Those sacred words in our constitution must not be equivocated.

In the Pledge Allegiance to this great country of ours, it ends with the phrase, *"with liberty and justice for all."*

There has been much debate as to whether or not the pledge should be recited in our public schools and at athletic events because it contains the phrase *"One Nation under God."*

The controversy <u>should</u> be over the phrase, *"with liberty and justice for all."* because that has proven not to be true throughout time, but there is no where in the pledge where it specifies who's or what God.

It is all about Human Rights.

It really does start with the individual, each and every one of us.

The United Shades of America is a Faith based initiative that will certainly not solve all of America's woes. That was not the intent.

My hope is that it will help facilitate our efforts to treat each other with more respect and for other countries to view the United States of America in a more positive light.

A great desire I had was to speak to all of the youth and citizens of America. If I had that opportunity, I just said what I would say!

Operation Peace and Brotherhood

"There is a rose in the fisted glove,

And the eagle flies with the dove..."

Peace and Brotherhood

It's not just an act, it's an attitude!

What the Symbol means

It is an International Symbol of Peace
It is a Personal Symbol of Peace

Many countries believe that it is the United States of America who has had the "clinched fist" of aggression and suppression for so many years, and if we are honest with ourselves, they may be right.

The United States of America is a powerful, progressive country, and there are times when our "might was right".

There were (are) times also, where we were wrong in our actions.

We must learn from our mistakes, move on and never repeat them again.

In that sense, we *must* clinch our fists and remain a strong world leader.

In that clinched fist though, there should be a rose, not a weapon or the threat of violence toward each other or other countries.

The Rose in the Fisted Glove on the symbol represents forgiveness, and the peace and love that we need to extend to one another, and to other countries.

The Eagle flying with the Dove represents the urgent need for the United States of America to take the lead in helping other countries to increase peace, equality and stability all around the world.

The Eagle represents the United States, and the Dove is a symbol of Peace.

The background for the images is the planet Earth.

It is my desire that *Operation Peace and Brotherhood* will touch the hearts, souls and minds of people all around the world.

It is a personal symbol of peace for me also, because for so many years I had a "clinched fist", fueled by social injustices that I had encountered in my own life. It produced bitterness and hatred.

My fist is still clinched; expressing the passion that I have for Peace and Brotherhood, but the bitterness and hatred is now replaced by the Rose in the Fisted Glove. I now know that harboring bitterness and hatred is self-destructive, and also hurts many other innocent people.

But it can be overcome!

What It Is

It is an effort to help identify and rectify the negative acts and attitudes that have prevented us all from treating each other with dignity and respect.

Whenever countries take military action against one another, the modern term for that action is often dubbed, an *"operation"*. Operation Desert Storm, Operation Desert Shield, and Operation Enduring Freedom are all a part of our recent history and memory.

The *"Operations"* that I just identified, were led by The United States of America. I am a proud veteran, and I will always support our troops regardless of the circumstances or destinations of their deployment.

It cannot be denied though, that the *"Operations"* that we have engaged in the past two decades, particularly in the Middle East, have not always been clearly defined, and have created more enemies than friends.

We have advocated freedom and democracy, and used that as a reason to invade and occupy other countries, while we do not even extend the full benefits of the two, to our own fellow citizens and neighbors.

That is a harsh truth that we must not deny any longer.

We must stop the favoritism, nepotism, narcissism, and the greedy attitudes that are so prevalent today in our society, all the way from Washington D.C. to Wall Street, to Main Street, to OUR streets!

We all must be willing to talk/listen to one another in understanding.

We all must have the capacity to disagree without being disagreeable.

Other countries are aware of the double-standard in our country also, and that helps to fuel their deep belief that the United States of America is an arrogant, dualistic and imperialistic country.

Whether those views are justified or not, we can no longer ignore those who have different views or cultures than us, or those whom we deem our *"enemy"*.

Our current President had this message for the leaders in the Middle East, *"we will extend a hand if you are willing to unclench your fist."*

That (this) can be a watershed moment in our quest for Peace and Brotherhood, at home and abroad.

Operation Peace and Brotherhood is a Faith based initiative with a simple mission; to help us all understand that Peace and Brotherhood is not just an act, it's an attitude!

Why the Operation was created

I want to not only help spread Peace and Brotherhood throughout our own communities, states, and country, but all around the world too.

There is so much hatred and bitterness in the country and world today that it has almost become accepted as the norm.

There is nothing normal about it, and we as individuals have the ability to change that reality.

I would like for this *"Operation"* and symbol to reflect to people all around the world, that the United States of America is serious about trying to promote peace and brotherhood at home and abroad.

I would also like this *"Operation"* and symbol to reflect to people all over the world that the United States of America is not just about politicians and their sometimes self-serving political agendas, and greedy, indulgent executives and business leaders; but about caring, faith filled, forgiving, and passionate people too.

I must confess that much of the passion behind this *"Operation"* and symbol was also fueled by the own hatred and bitterness that I had harbored for so many years.

It was only through faith and understanding that I was able to let go of my hatred and bitterness, and begin to really care and forgive once again.

When I was a child, there was a special girl in our neighborhood who mentored to all of the other children.

She played church and school with us. She taught us a lot about the value of life.

One of the things that made her special was that she was born with a heart condition.

The doctors who delivered her didn't think she would live past the age of five.

When that special girl was twelve-years old, because she was different, a group of girls viciously beat her head into a concrete wall, paralyzing her and leaving her speechless. She passed away two years later in a nursing home at the age of fourteen.
I was eight-years old.
I went to the nursing home and read to her the last two years of her life. I love and miss that special girl. That special girl was my oldest sister.

When I was a child, there was a young boy in the neighborhood who would always play catch with me.

We would play catch and talk for hours at a time. We did practically everything together. He was my best friend.

When he was fourteen-years old, someone intentionally put poison in a soft drink bottle, and he drank it, and after much intense pain and suffering, he died two days later. I never got a chance to say goodbye to him. I was thirteen-years old.

There was so much that we talked about at night and still needed to say. I love and miss my best friend. My best friend was my brother, born on Christmas Day.

Those events changed my family's life forever. My innocence was lost.

The seeds of hatred and bitterness were planted in my heart.

Overcoming Hatred and Bitterness

It would be wonderful if we could wave a magic wand and make all of the hatred and bitterness in the world just disappears.

It is not that simple however; not only do we have to address the situation or circumstances that caused the hatred and bitterness in the first place, but we must also understand the metamorphosis of the two.

It really comes down to treating others the way that you want to be treated.

I can not, nor will I try to explain the bitterness and hatred that I had harbored over the losses of my Brother and Sister, and the circumstances behind their deaths.

There is no need to wallow anymore in sorrow and self-pity, because I know that so many of my fellow citizens, and in fact, people all around the world unfortunately still are going through social injustices such as my family and I have endured, and harbor the same hatred and bitterness that I once held for so many years.

By harboring those feelings though, I realize now that I too had been paralyzed, and had poison coursing through my own veins. But the poison was hatred and bitterness, not arsenic, and the paralysis was of my own volition by not choosing Faith over fear.

I could not reach the effectiveness and happiness that I wanted in my own life until I changed my attitude and heart.

That certainly was not an easy task, and there were many, many trials and tribulations along the way.

The change only came about through Faith and understanding.

The Faith of a Mother
A Personal Testimony from a Son

I speak of Faith because it is what has enabled me to let go of all of the hatred and bitterness that I had held in my heart over the perceived or actual social injustices that I have encountered in my life time.

Faith is one of the essential elements of our lives that my siblings and I were raised with, but it was often just taken for granted or maybe not even acknowledged much at all.

My Mother and two of my Great-Aunts founded a church in my hometown, at the mid-point of the last century.

Church services were initially held in a home until, through Faith and hard work, a Church was constructed.

My Mother has Faith!

My Mother raised my siblings and me to always have Faith, and for the most part I think that we always did, even if it was typically fledging at times.

My Mother always has exhibited Faith, not only with her words, or lack of, but most importantly with her actions.

It is very easy for a son or child to be complimentary and biased towards their parent(s) (please help our young today), but under these circumstances, you must please overlook my obvious bias that I show toward my Mother to fully appreciate the Faith that she has given to me.

I have told you that I have lost a Sister and a Brother under very diabolic circumstances.

It is often said that the worst thing in life is losing a child.

My Mother is and was a widow when she lost her Daughter and Son. My Mother showed Faith! My Mother NEVER said an angry word! My Mother said we must move on because they were in a better place.

My Mother has shown grace and dignity equal to Jaclyn Kennedy Onassis and Coretta Scott King, and it should be known to all!

My Mother never struck me or said an angry word to me.

My Mother provided stability and structure in our home.

My Mother gave me life before I lost my brother and sister. My Mother gave me my life back after I lost my brother and sister.

My Mother gave me Faith once again!

It's a Miracle...

My Mother taught my siblings and me how to treat other people, not only with her words, but more importantly, with her actions.

My Mother worked for the State, and encountered people from all walks of life. My Mother has worked with nationally and internationally known people.

My Mother has worked with the very poor.

My Mother treated(s) everyone the same, no matter their social status. My Mother's actions created a passion in me for Civil and Human rights.

My Mother was born in the era of Dr. Martin Luther King Jr.

I have always admired the principles that Dr. King stood for.

Dr. King believed in a personal God and the redemptive power of love.

Dr. King believed that you should love yourself, love your neighbor as you love yourself, and love your Lord with all of your heart in order to live a complete life.

Dr. King helped to inspire my passion for Peace and Brotherhood.

The World is a ball of confusion right now.

The United States of America has some very serious issues that must be addressed with urgency.

I am one of the millions of Americans who has lost their job within the past year.

I am one of the millions of Americans who go through daily trials and tribulations in and out of the home.

I was experiencing heavy tribulation on the eve of Dr. King's birthday recently, and I said a heart-felt prayer to my God...

"Heavenly father I know you are real. I have Faith, but sometimes I am weak. I am weak right now. Will you please show me a Miracle so that I can know that you are still with me?"

I felt better after I said the prayer, but I was still weak. Dr. King's birthday was the next day.

As I sat watching Sports Center, the phone rang. My Mother was calling me.

My Mother told me an airplane had crashed into the Hudson River.

My Mother and I watched as the passengers walked out onto the wings of love unscathed, all alive! My Mother said, *"Isn't that an absolute Miracle?!"*

My God showed me a Miracle, My Mother told me of a Miracle...

The passengers were literally walking on water, and all were safe and alive.

I don't know their names or where they were from, it doesn't matter...

I just know that they all survived this Miracle, and that does matter!

The Captain does not realize that when he saved the passengers' lives, he helped save mine also.

Thank you sincerely from the bottom of my heart.

This is one reason that we must find the Faith, and keep the Faith.

Free at Last

My Mother spoke the word Miracle, and I was overcome with a wave of joy and excitement. I felt a Spirit passing through my body. I felt at peace. The hatred and bitterness that I had once held towards others replaced with empathy and love.

I felt such a sense of freedom.

The trials and tribulations that I have gone through in my life have been difficult and challenging, but I feel very blessed to have learned and grown in Faith through it all.

Without the pain and suffering, I may have never really understood the importance of Faith and become closer to my God.

I now know that the most important gift my Mother has ever given me is Faith.

I understand how difficult it is to have Faith in the world today.

There is too much hatred and bitterness.
There is so much greed.

There are so many different cultures and Religions.

There is even confusion about God's existence among scholars.

All I know is that I asked for a miracle and my God delivered for me.

He has continued to answer my prayers, bless me and put peace and love in my heart.

It doesn't matter whether you are a Catholic or a Protestant, a Jew or Gentile, when you pray to your God, if He puts peace and love in your heart, we have more in common than not.

One day the truth will be revealed to all of mankind.

I now see you as my Brother and Sister!

May my God answer your prayers and bless you too ...

Touching Letters

Thanks for the wonderful talk ~ you truly have a gift! It was a blessing to have you at N. Miami!

May the Lord continue to richly bless you!

6th Grade

I learned that no matter what color you are, you should be treated equal. That is why God made us that way. Some things that are interesting, when you came is you believe in in great freedom, and in all of us in what we do. Martin Luther King Jr belived in a lot of stuff that you do. I believe that if Martin did not do what he did then you would of. Thats how I know that you believe in great freedom, and all of us Monday, I took the time to think about what he did and why he did, then, and thats why I want to Thank you for coming to talk to us. Now I know and understand what he did and why. Thankyou again.

Your Friend,

Thanks for coming
to our school + talking to
us about Martin Luther King
Jr. I really enjoyed it. I never
thought about what Martin did that
way. I mean, I always thought
he just did for the colored peoples
rights. I never thought that it was
for everyone.

Thanks for showing
me how to
understand!

I wasn't here that day, but thank you for coming anyway. I think I would have enjoyed it. But I was in Orlando, having the time of my life. But, thanks anyway.

From, Harrison

4471887

Made in the USA
Lexington, KY
28 January 2010